Gemmusing Collection

Sunny Joiette
Comic raisonné: vol. 1

Copyright 2024
Victoria DesJardin

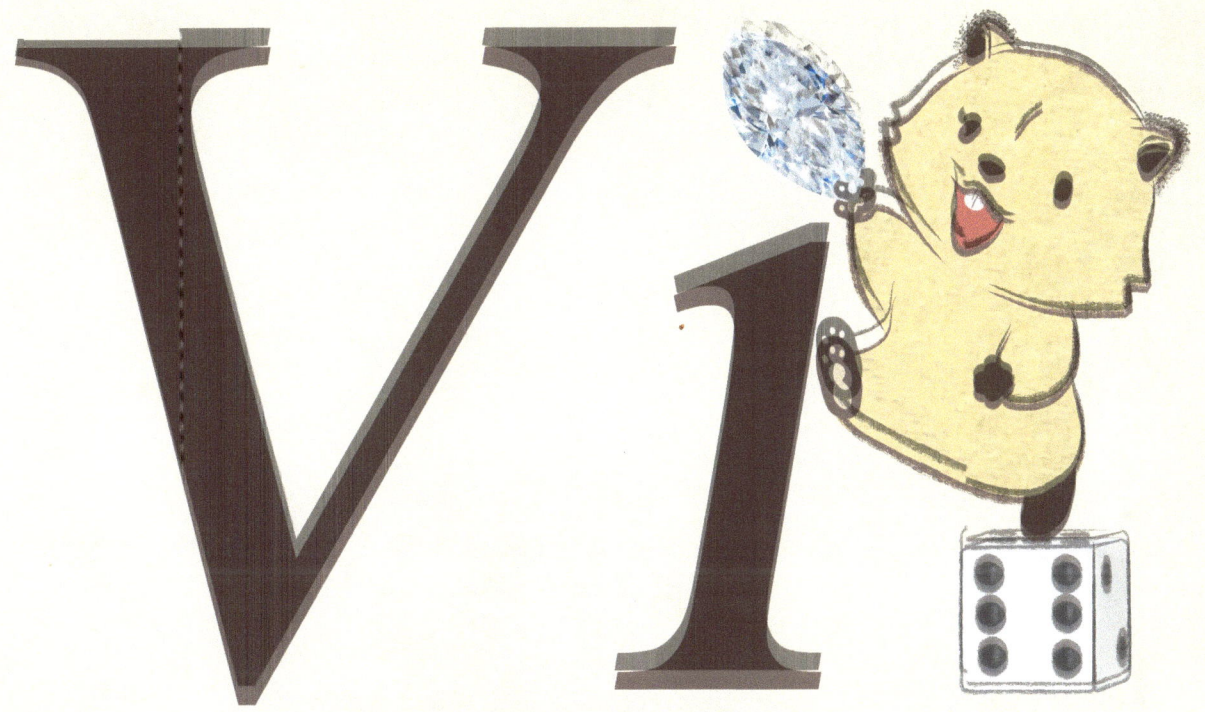

All rights reserved.
Unauthorized use is prohibited.
This book, or parts thereof, may not be reproduced in any form without written permission from the copyright owner.

~ *Atelier DesJardin* ~

atelierdesjardin@gmail.com

ISBN: 9798340053817

(**1**) (2) (3) (4) (5) (6) (7) (8) (9) (10) (11) (12)

Art Index

Ô Joy! ....pg 1

Edible Snowflake Ornaments ....pg 2

SEE Salt ....pg 3

Merry Meal: Evergreen Cupcake ....pg 4

Sweet Ride .... pg 5

Hang in There .... pg 6

Happy Dance .... pg 7

Warm Wishes .... pg 8

Chime In .... pg 9

Sparrow's Wintertime Jig .... pg 10

Creative Income: Cool Cash .... pg 11

Snow Angel .... pg 12

Sunny Joiette   two   *Comic raisonné: vol. 1*

Art Index

Have a nICE Day ....pg 13-14

Cool New Friend ....pg 15

FAUXcation: Vitamin SEA ....pg 16

Perfect PEAR ....pg 17

Sunny Loves to read .... pg 18

(BFF) Bunny Friend Forever .... pg 19

Snow Hoppy .... pg 20

Indoor Activités .... pg 21

Treat Tree .... pg 22

Let It Grow, Let It Grow, Let It Grow .... pg 23

ValenTHYMÉ .... pg 24

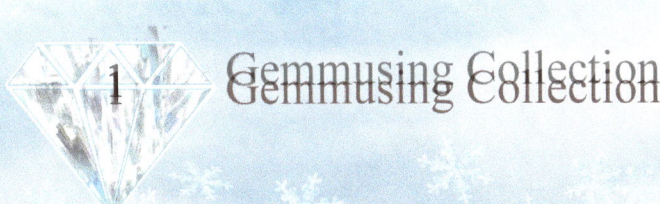

Gemmusing Collection 1

Sunny Joiette

Comic raisonné: vol. 1

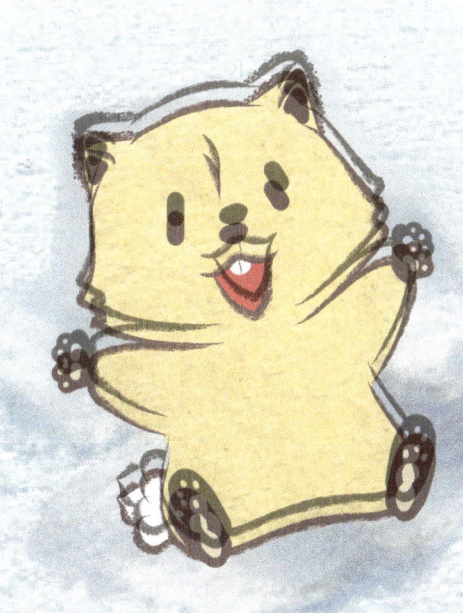

by Vi DesJardin

Gemmusing Collection

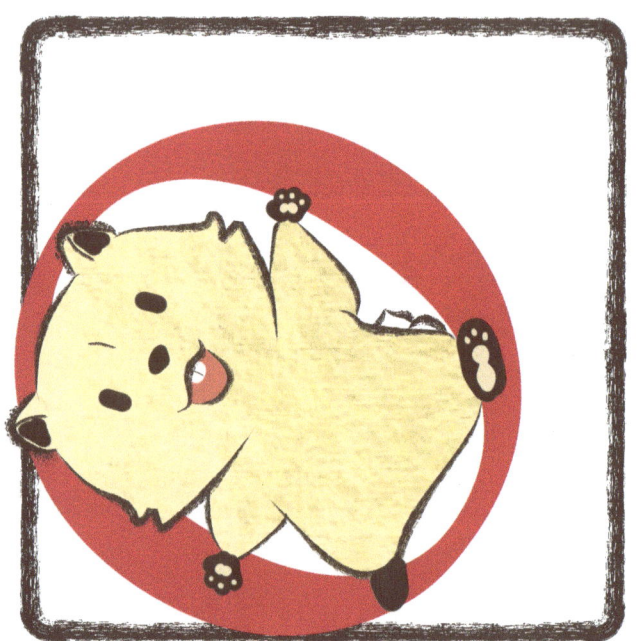
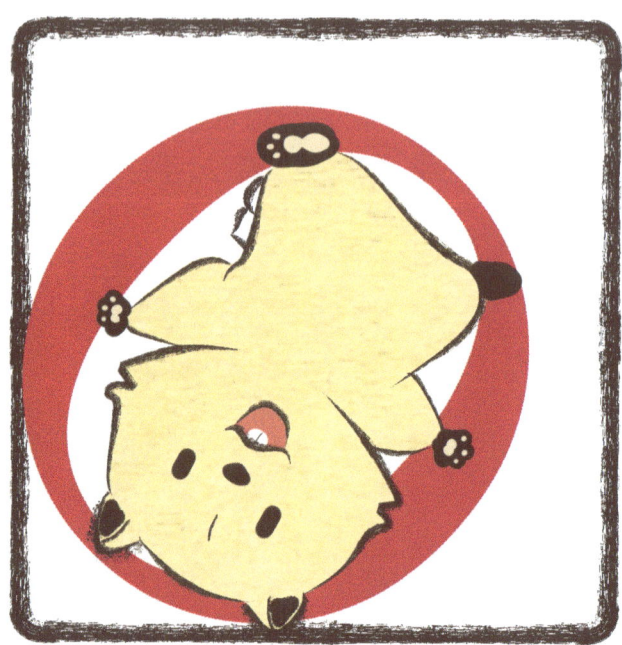
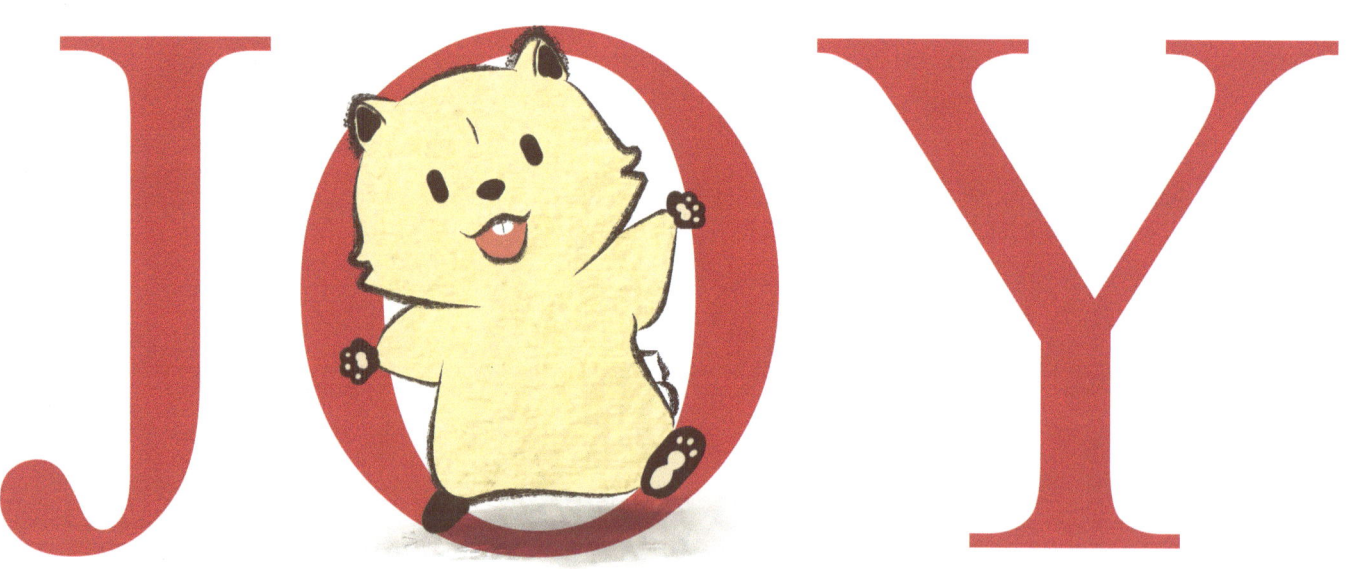

Sunny Joiette Comic raisonné: vol. 1

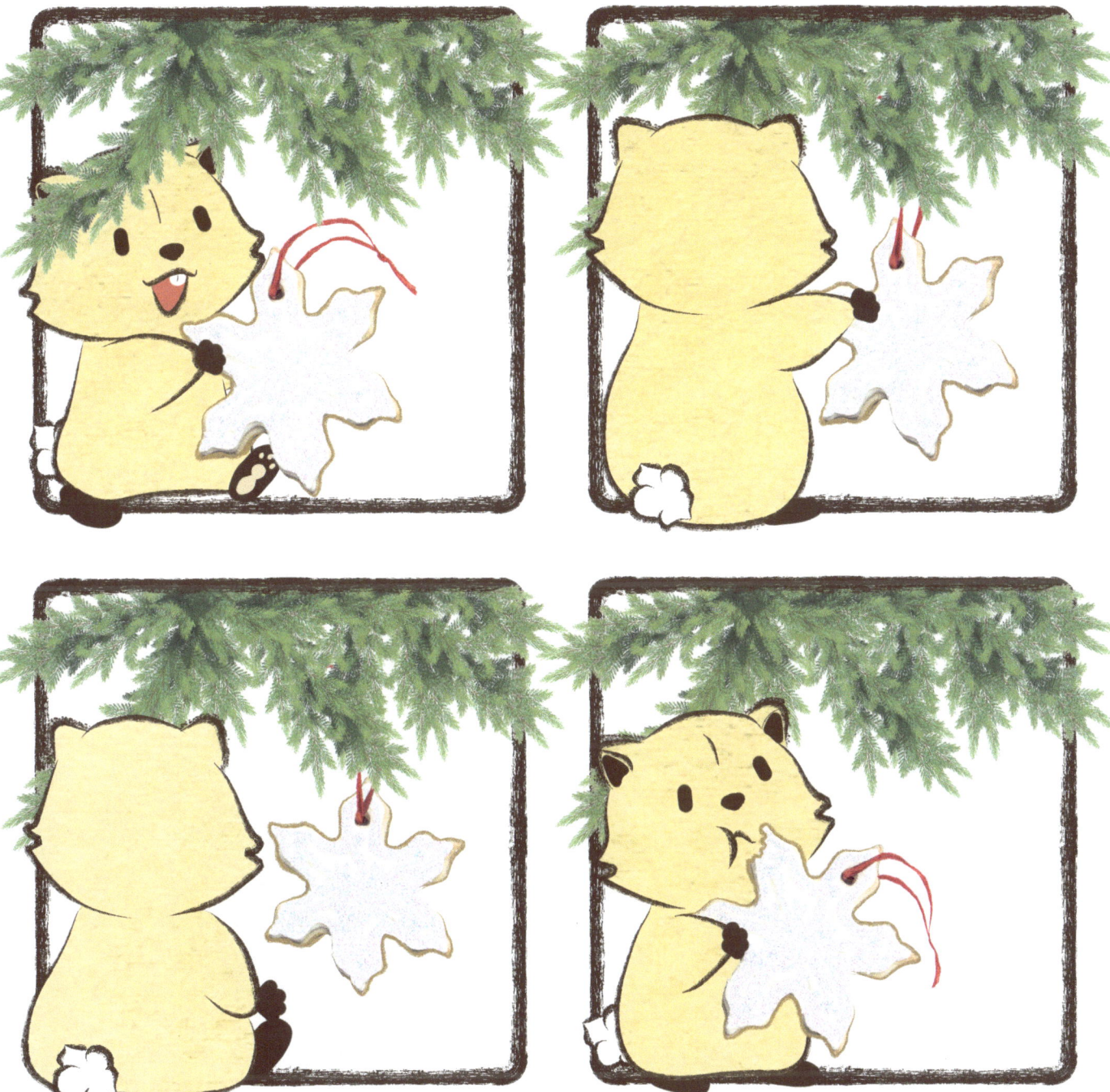

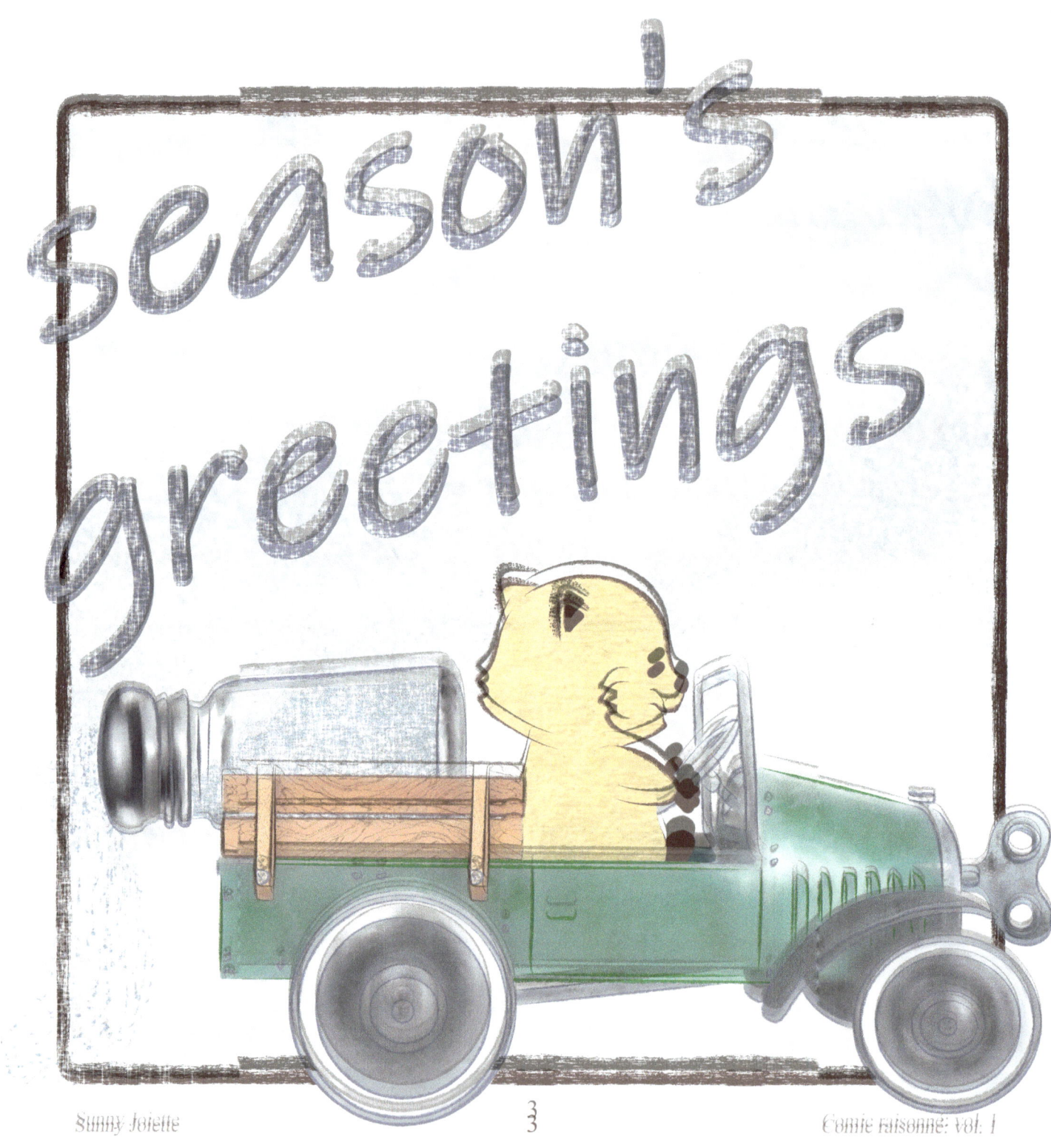

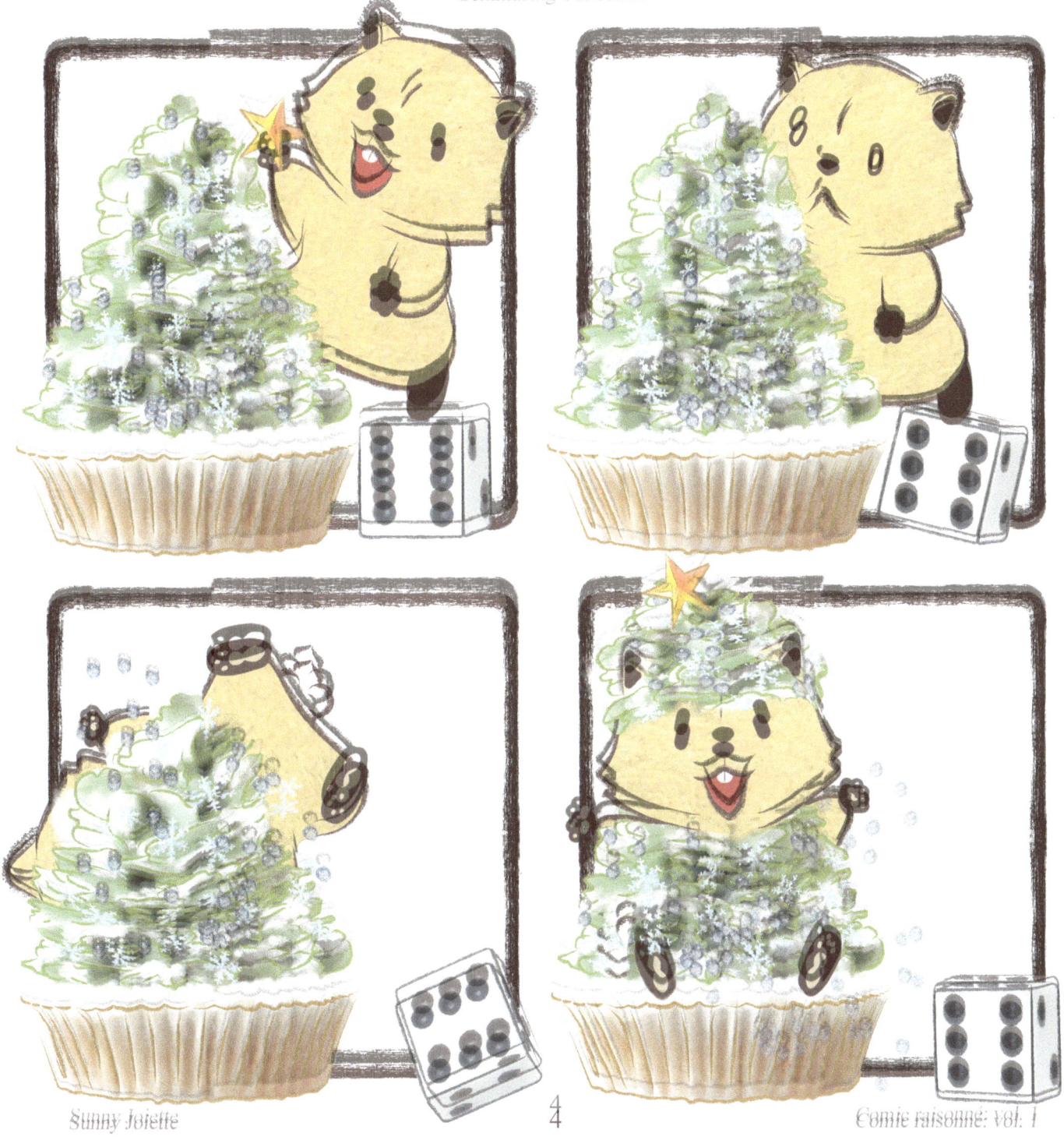

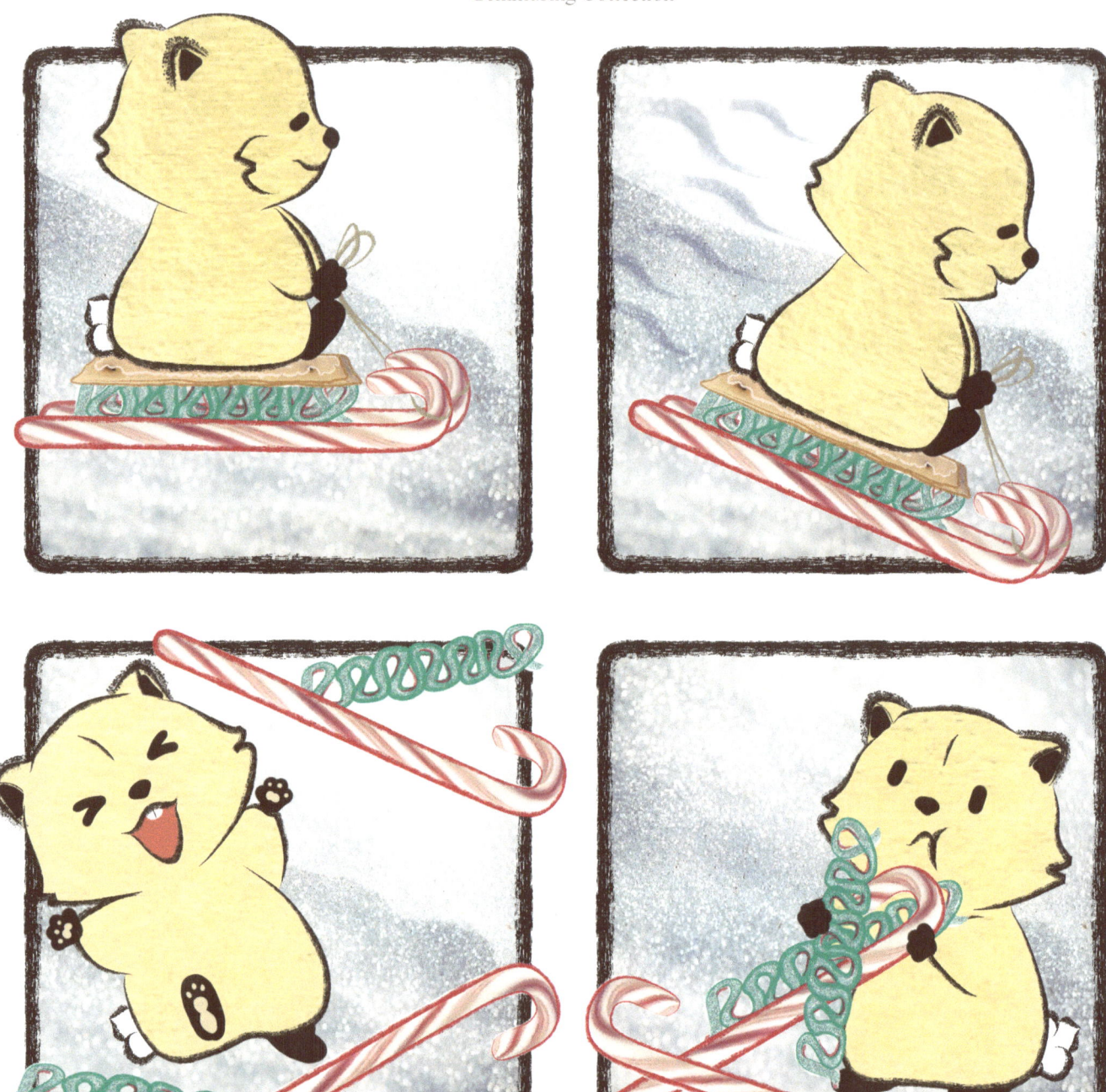

Gemmusing Collection

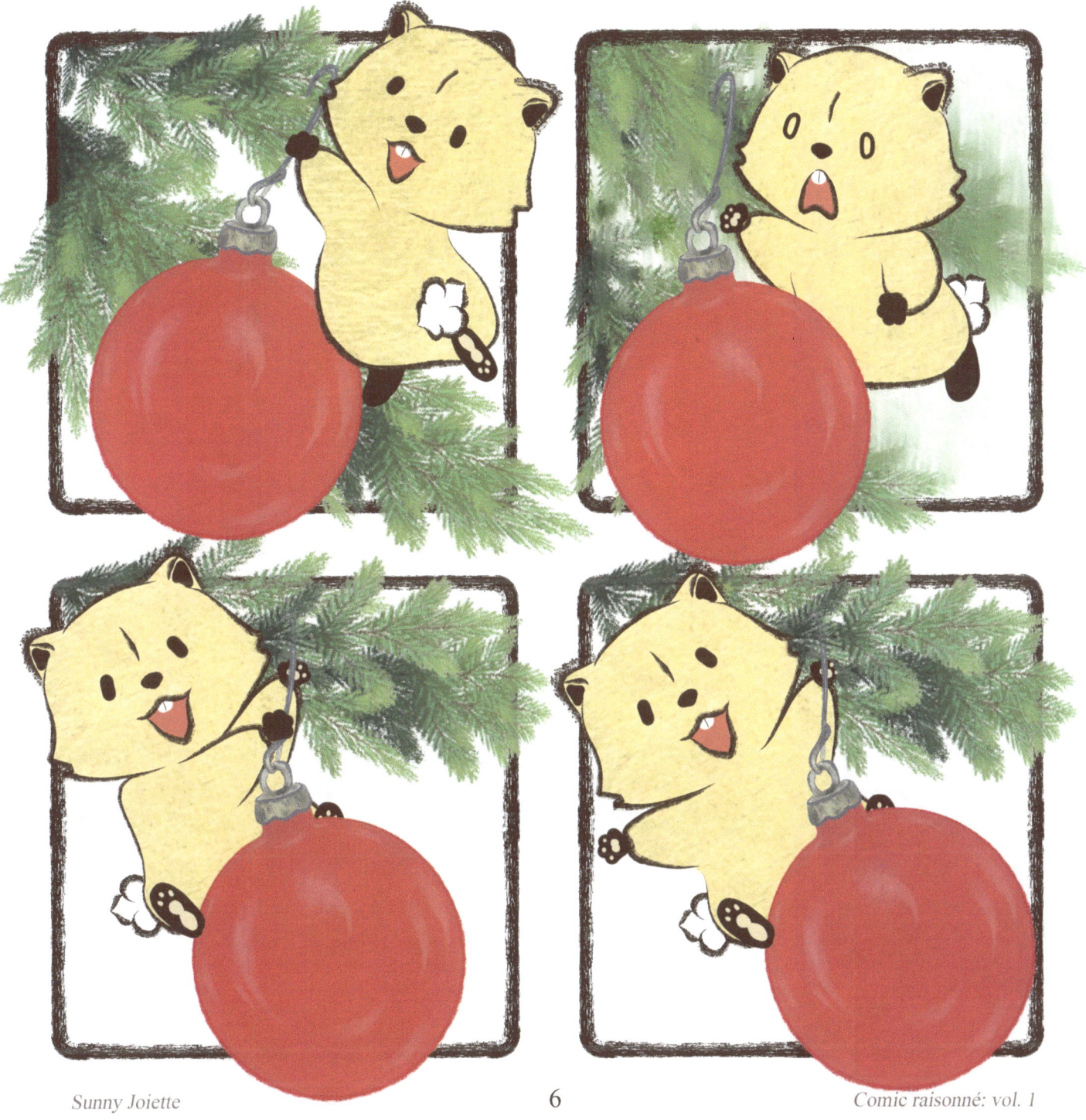

Sunny Joiette · Comic raisonné: vol. 1

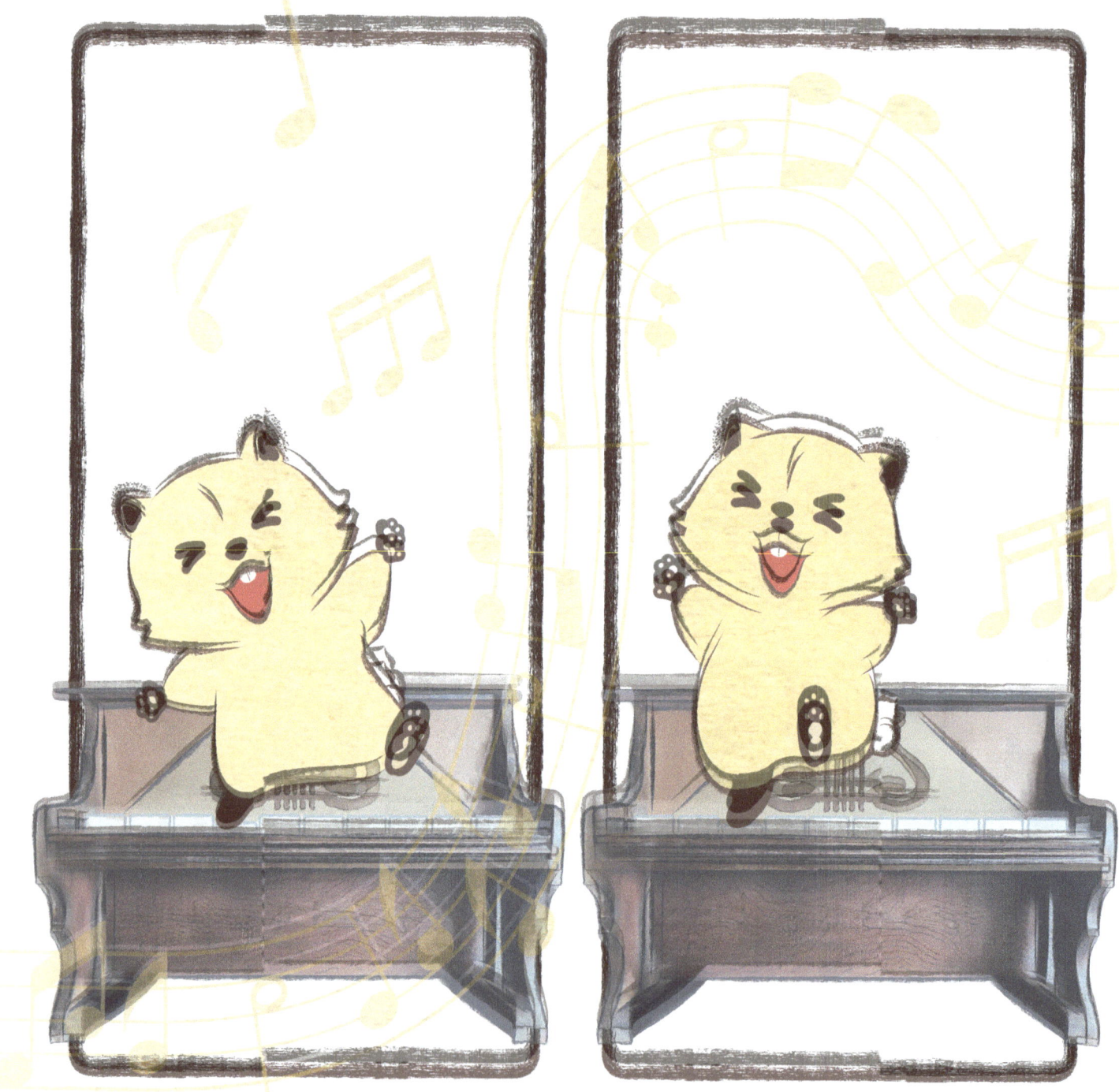

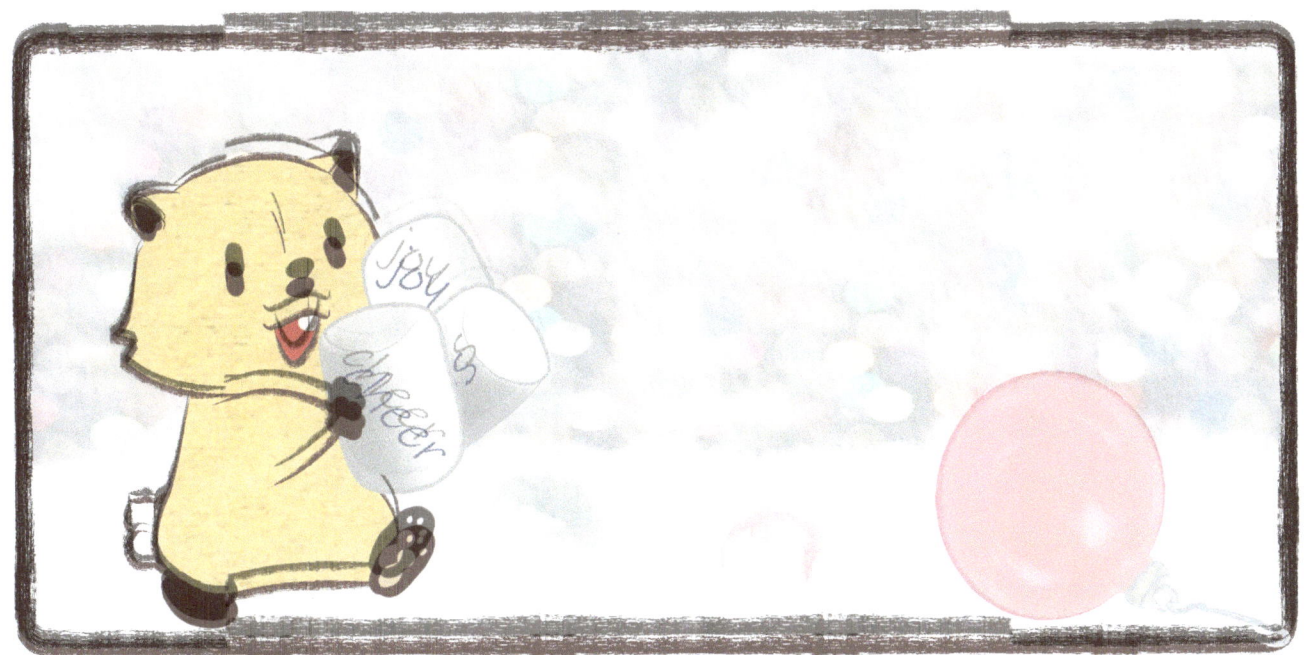
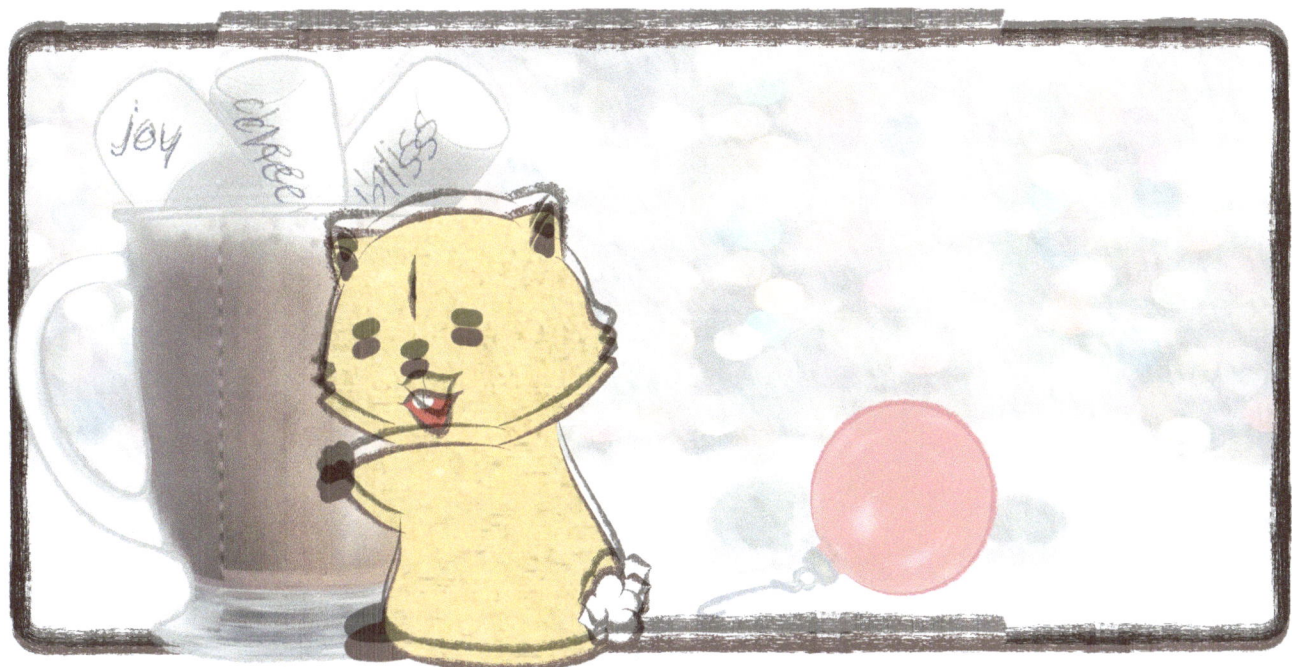

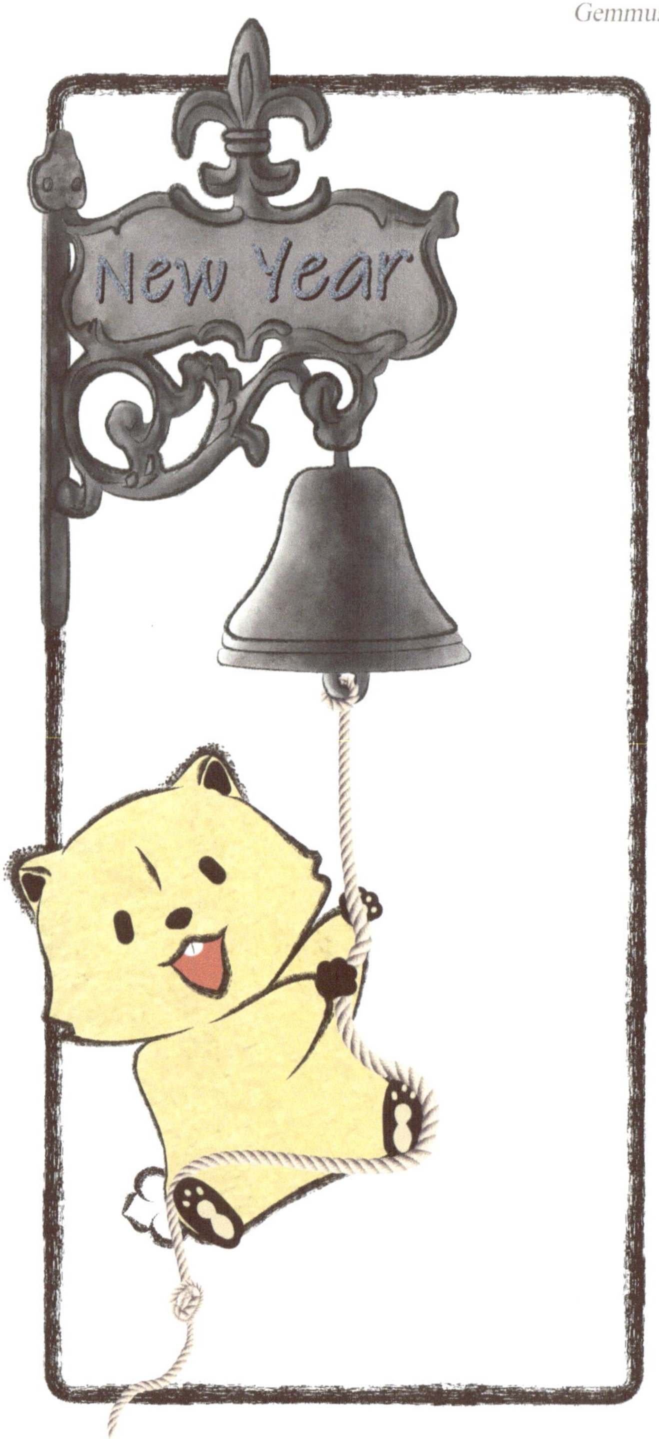

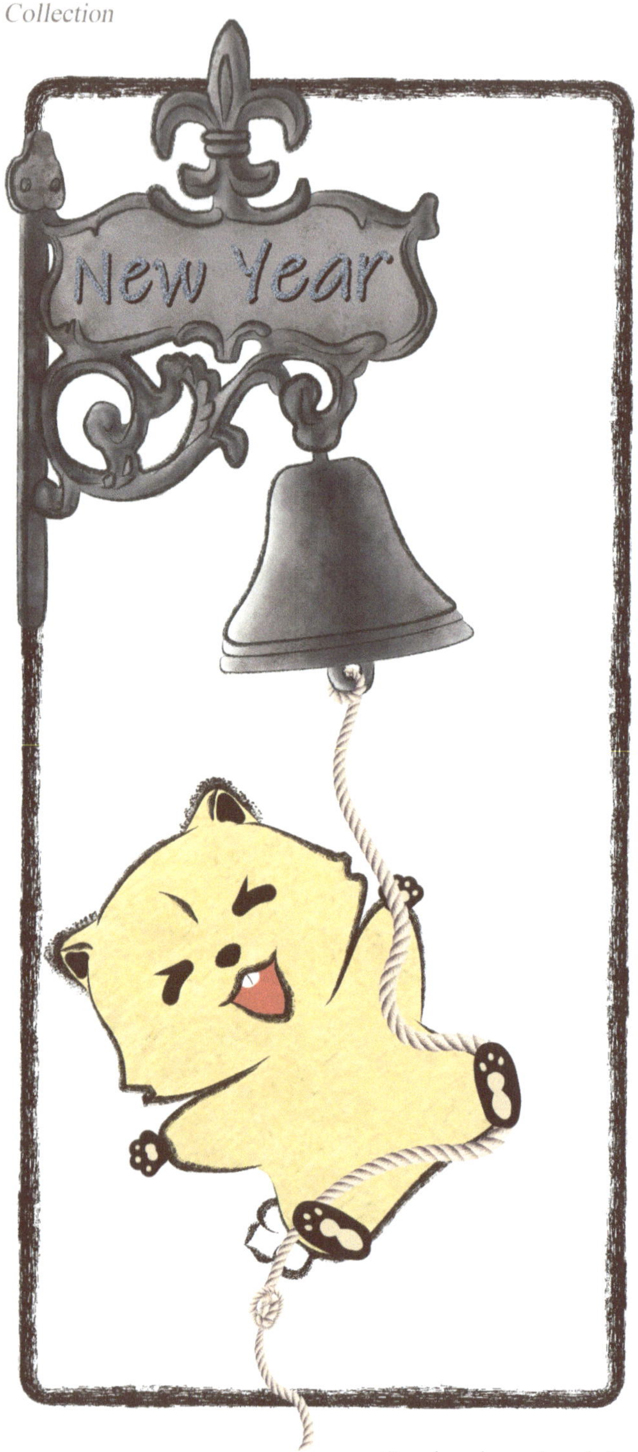

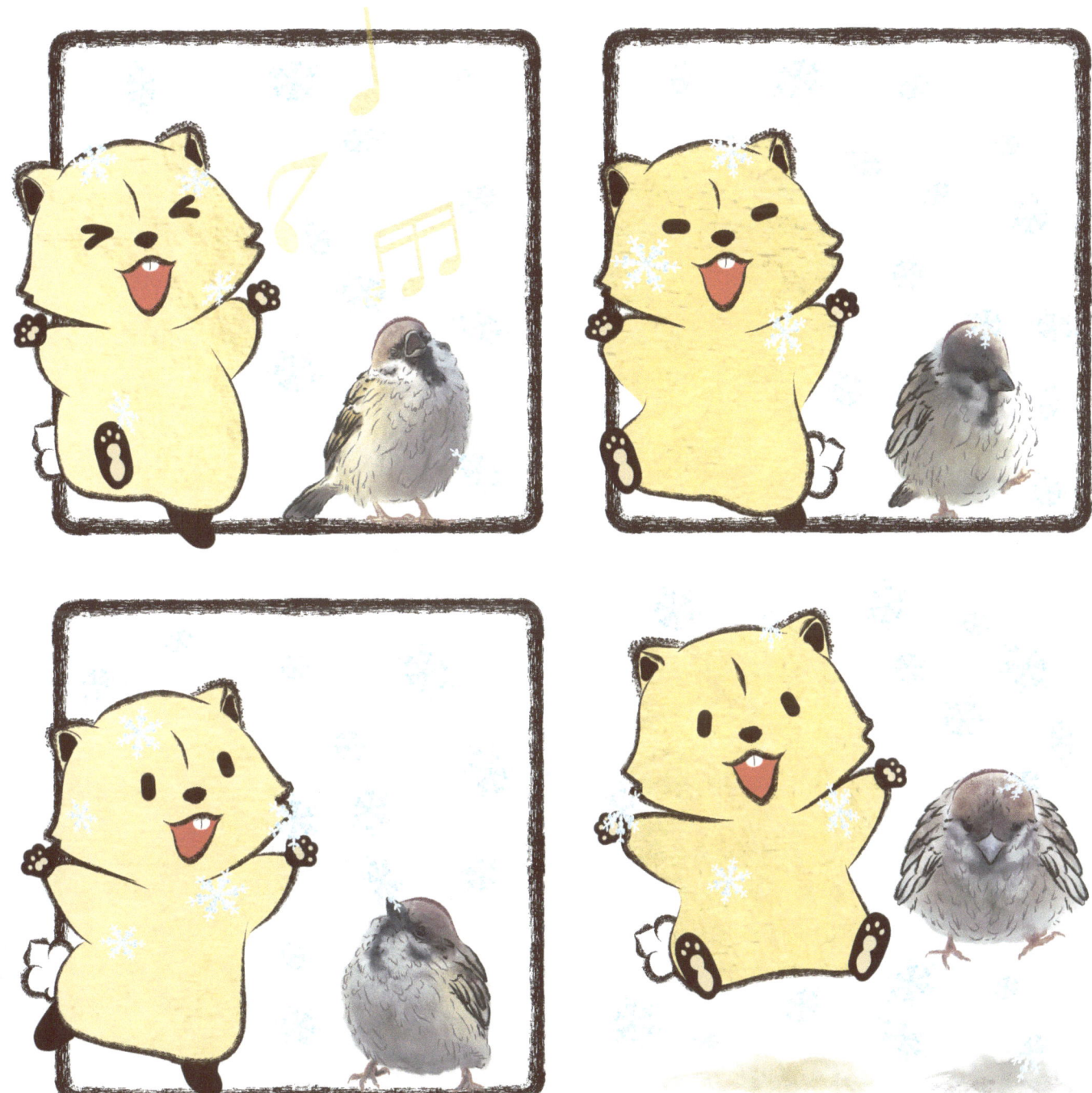

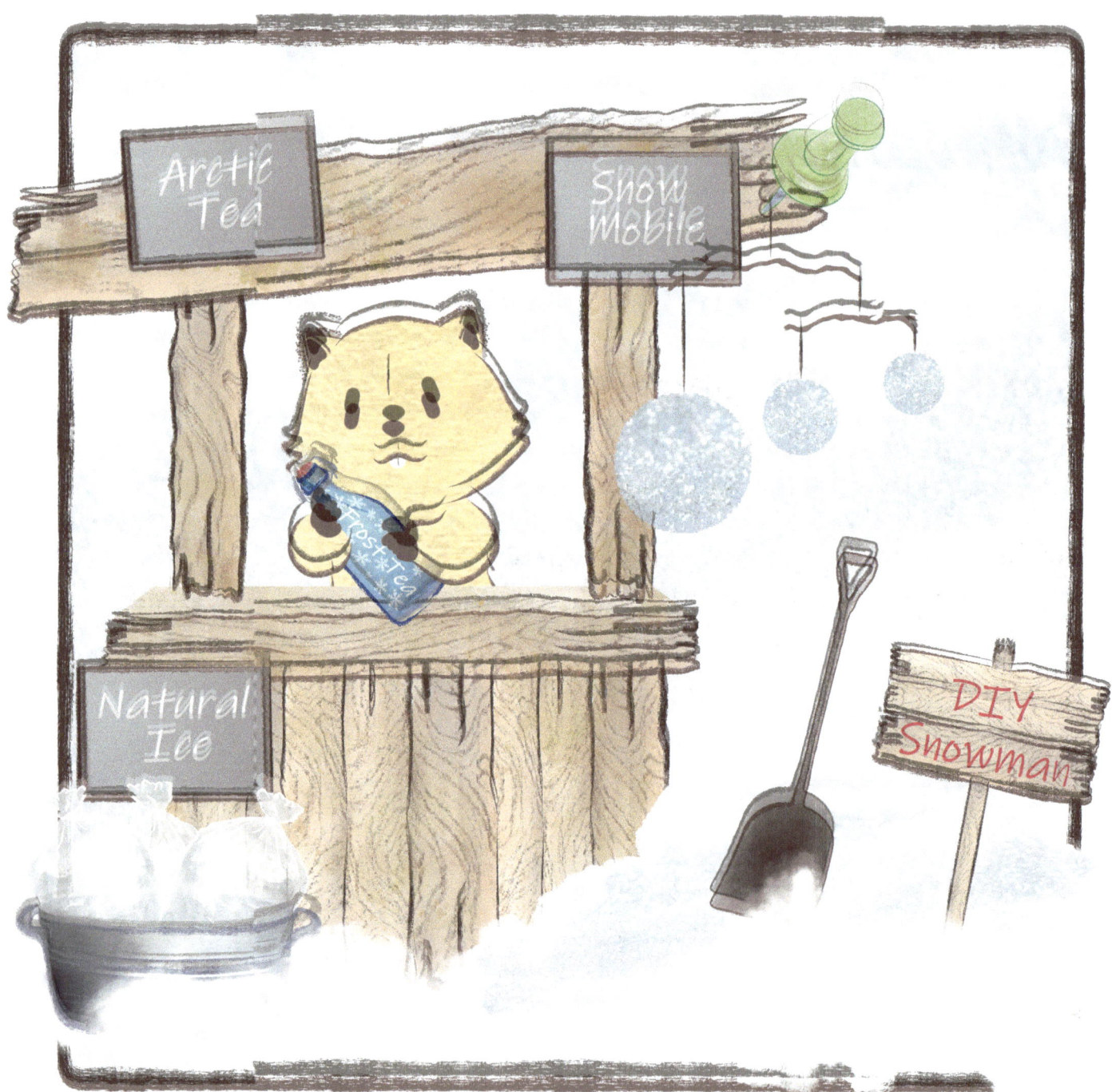

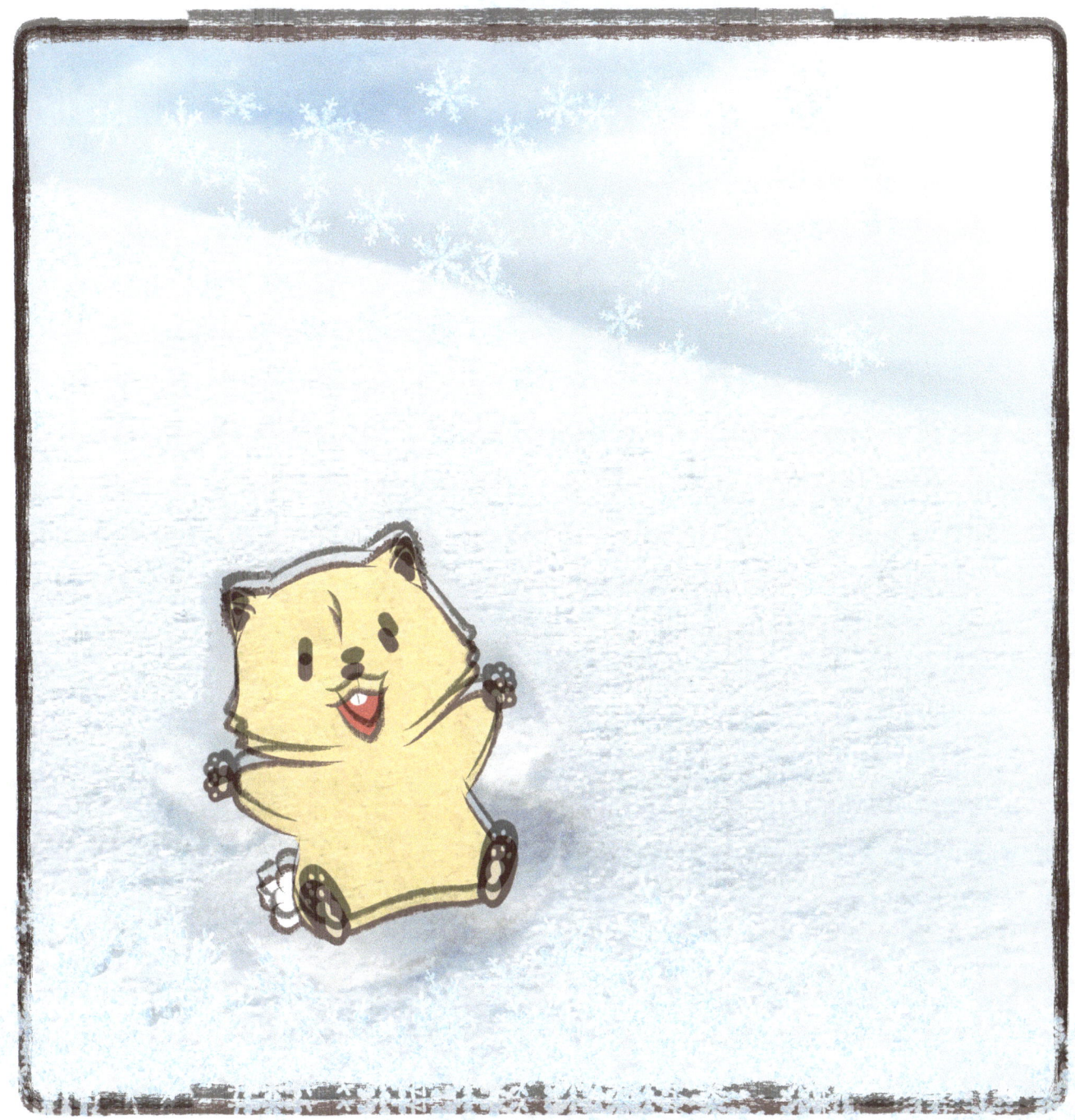

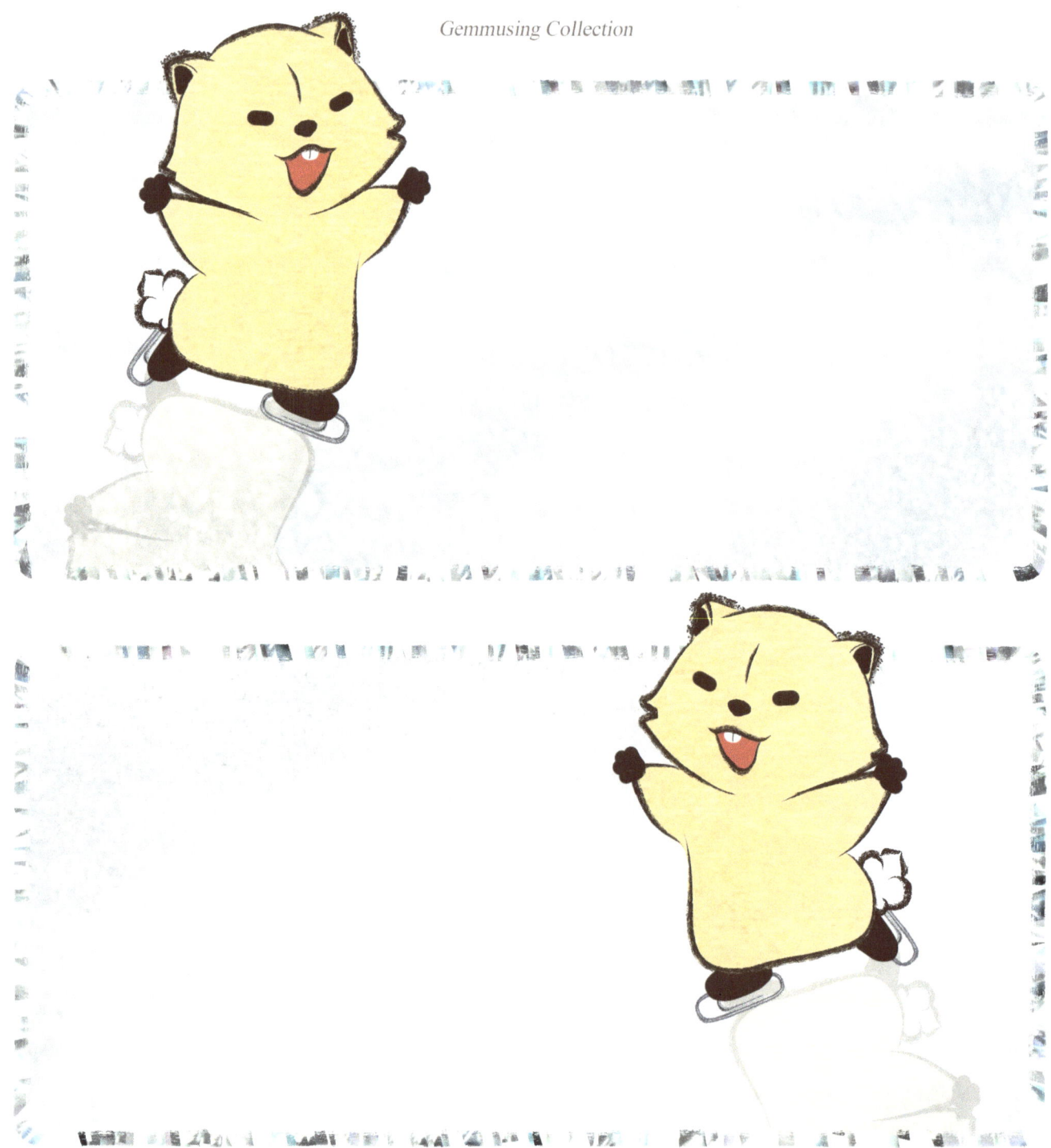

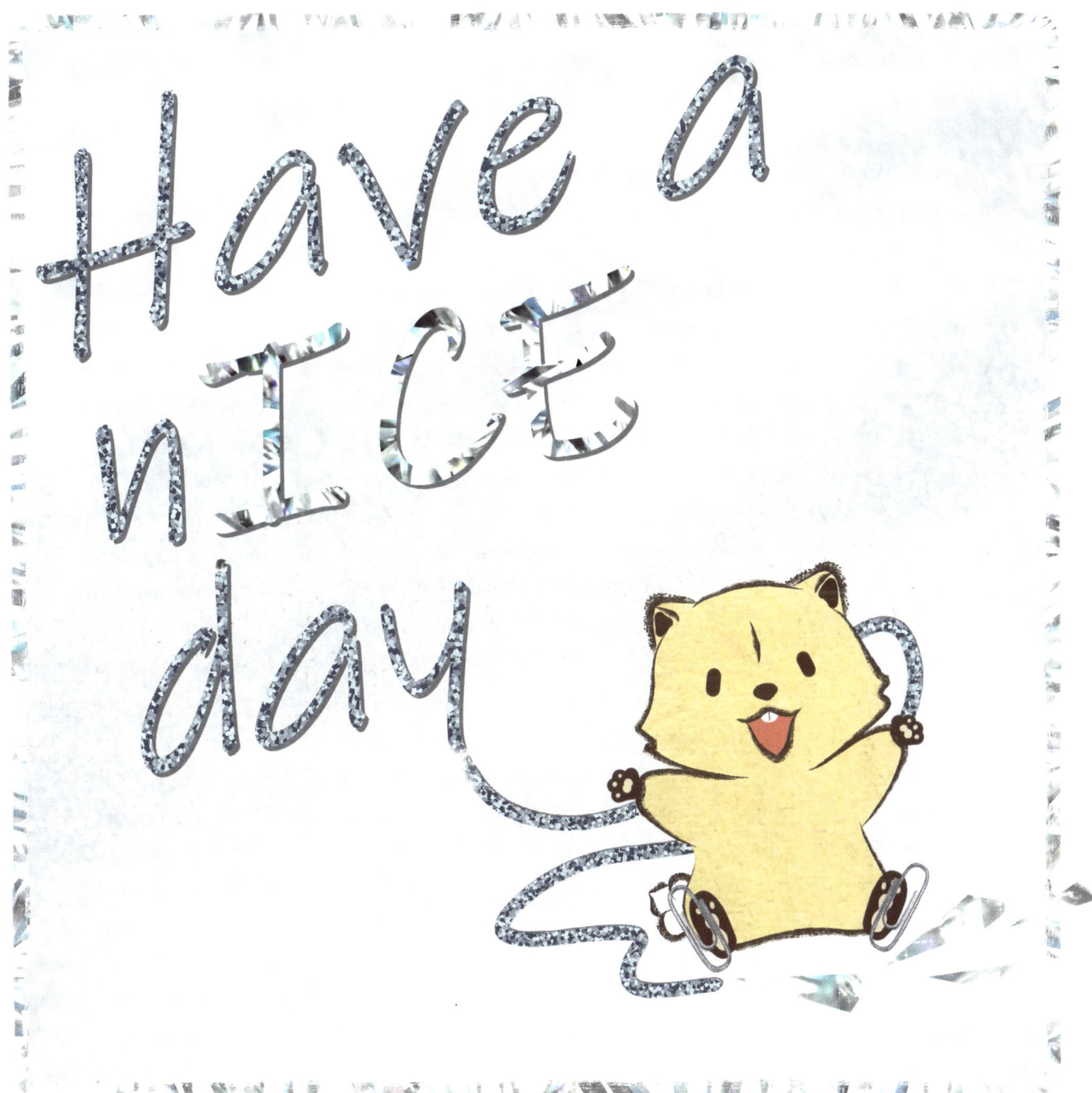

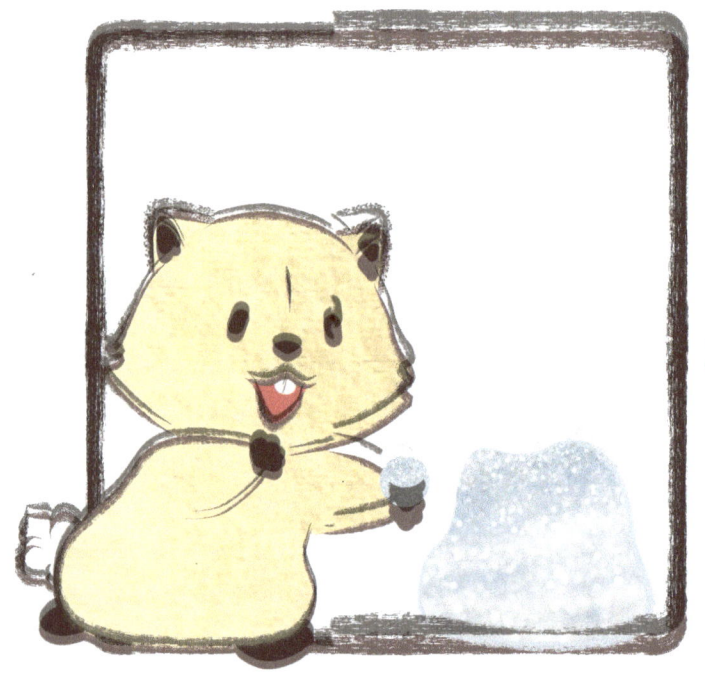
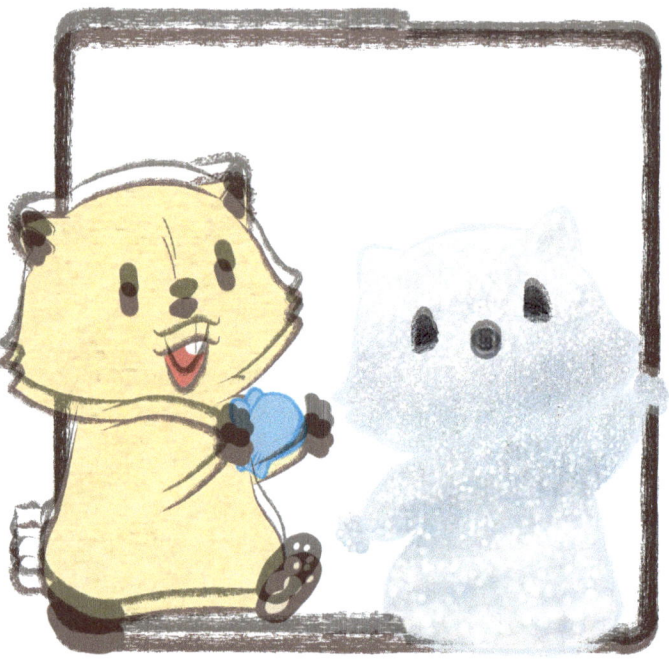

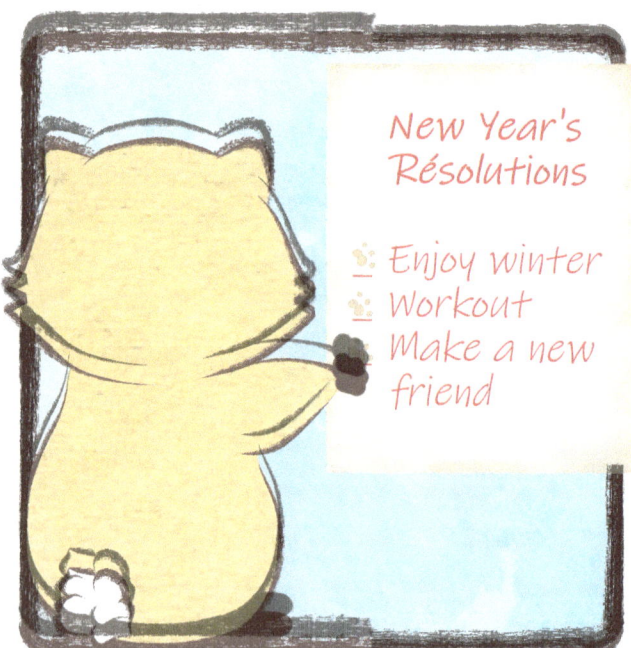

New Year's Résolutions

- Enjoy winter
- Workout
- Make a new friend

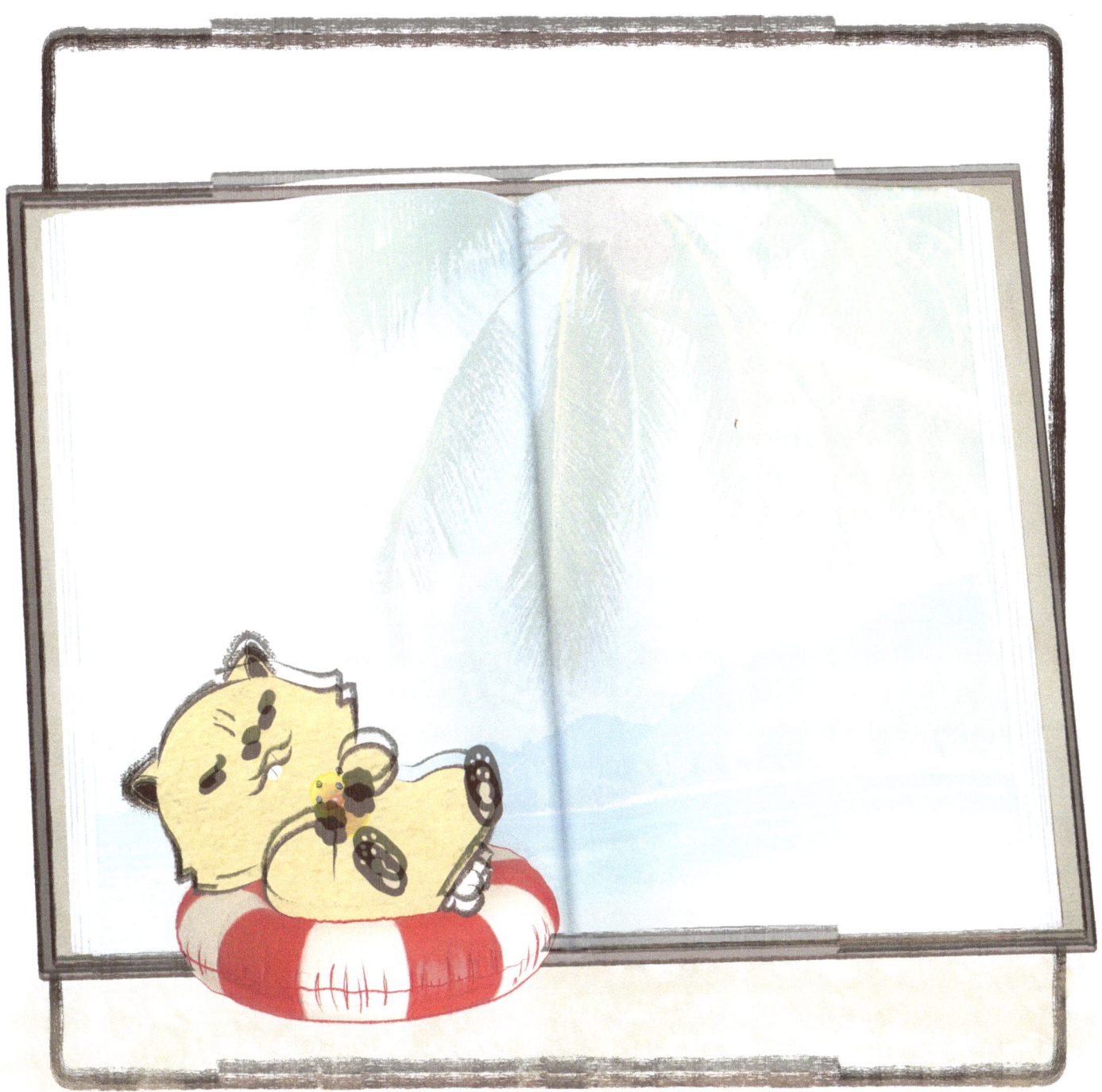

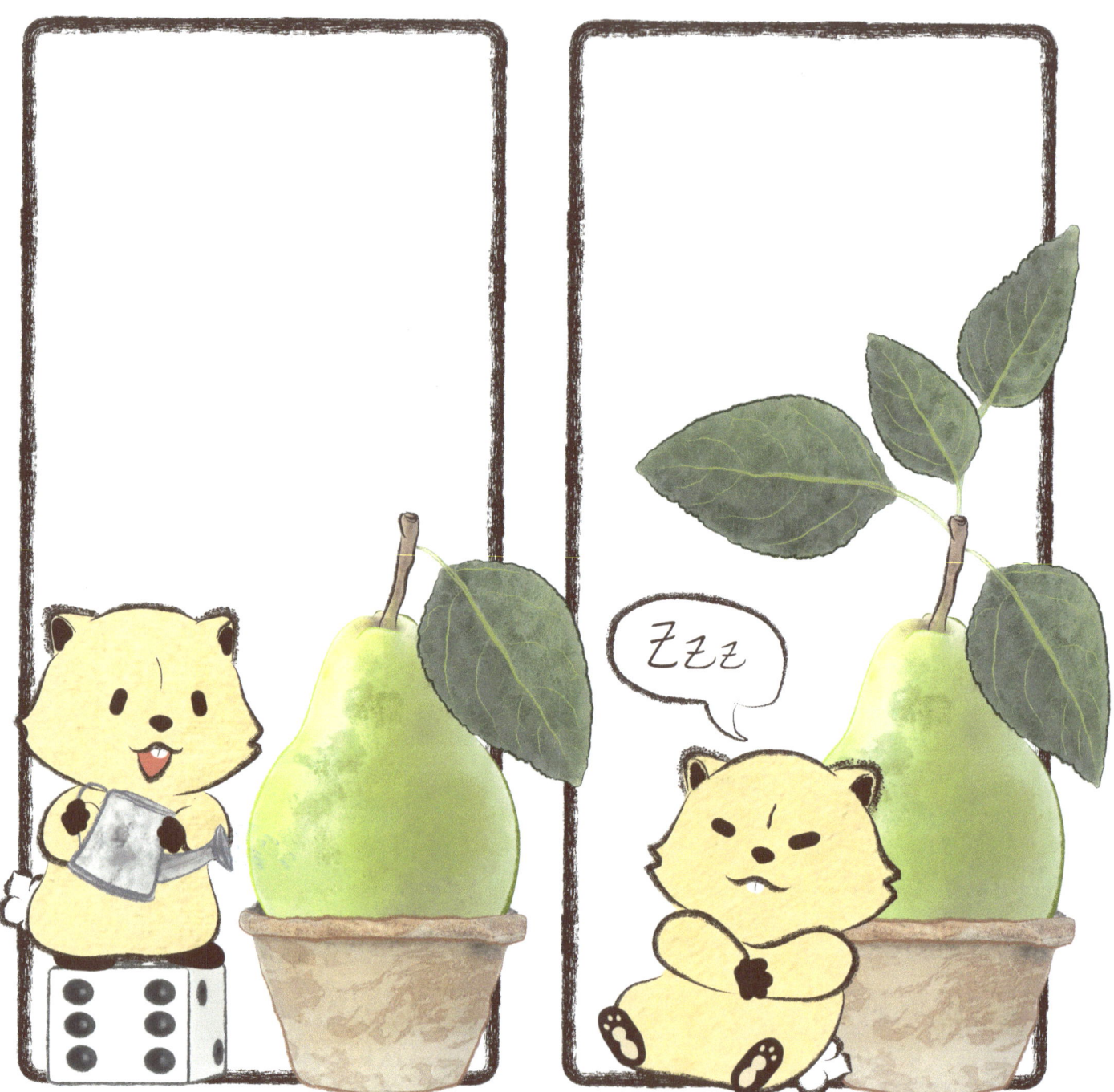

Gemmusing Collection

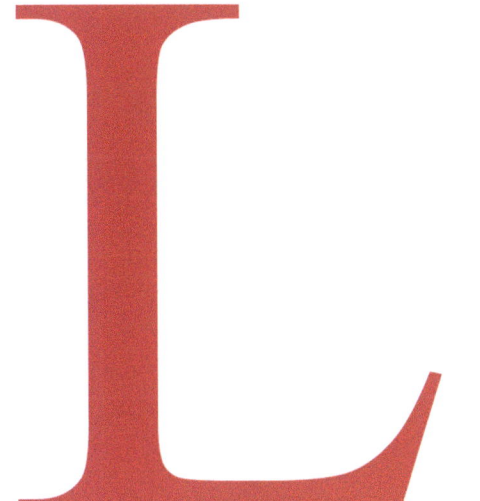 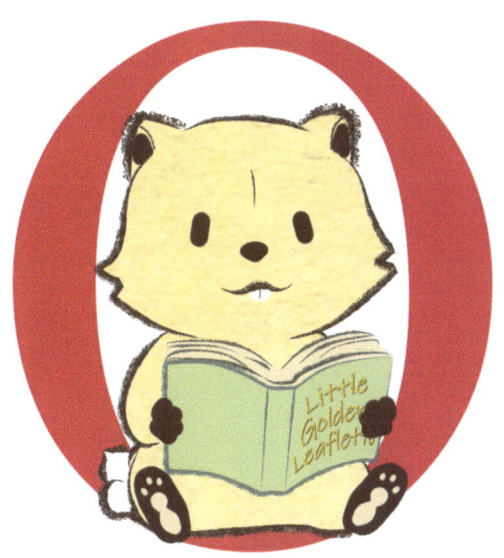

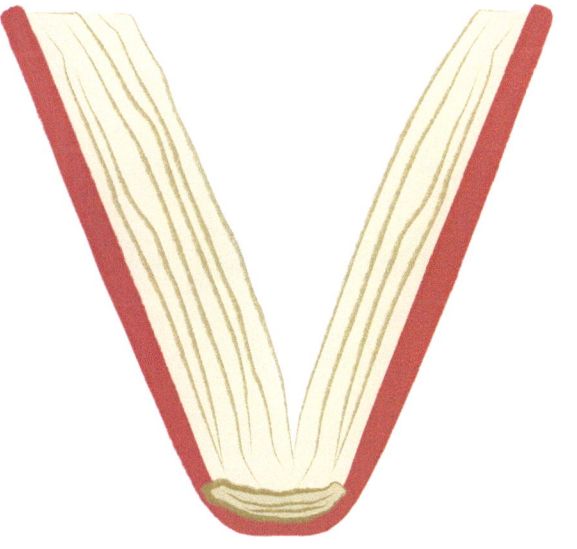 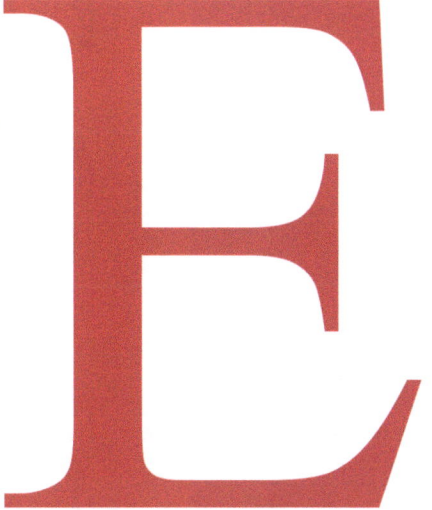

Sunny Joiette　　　　　　　　　　　　　　　　Comic raisonné: vol. 1

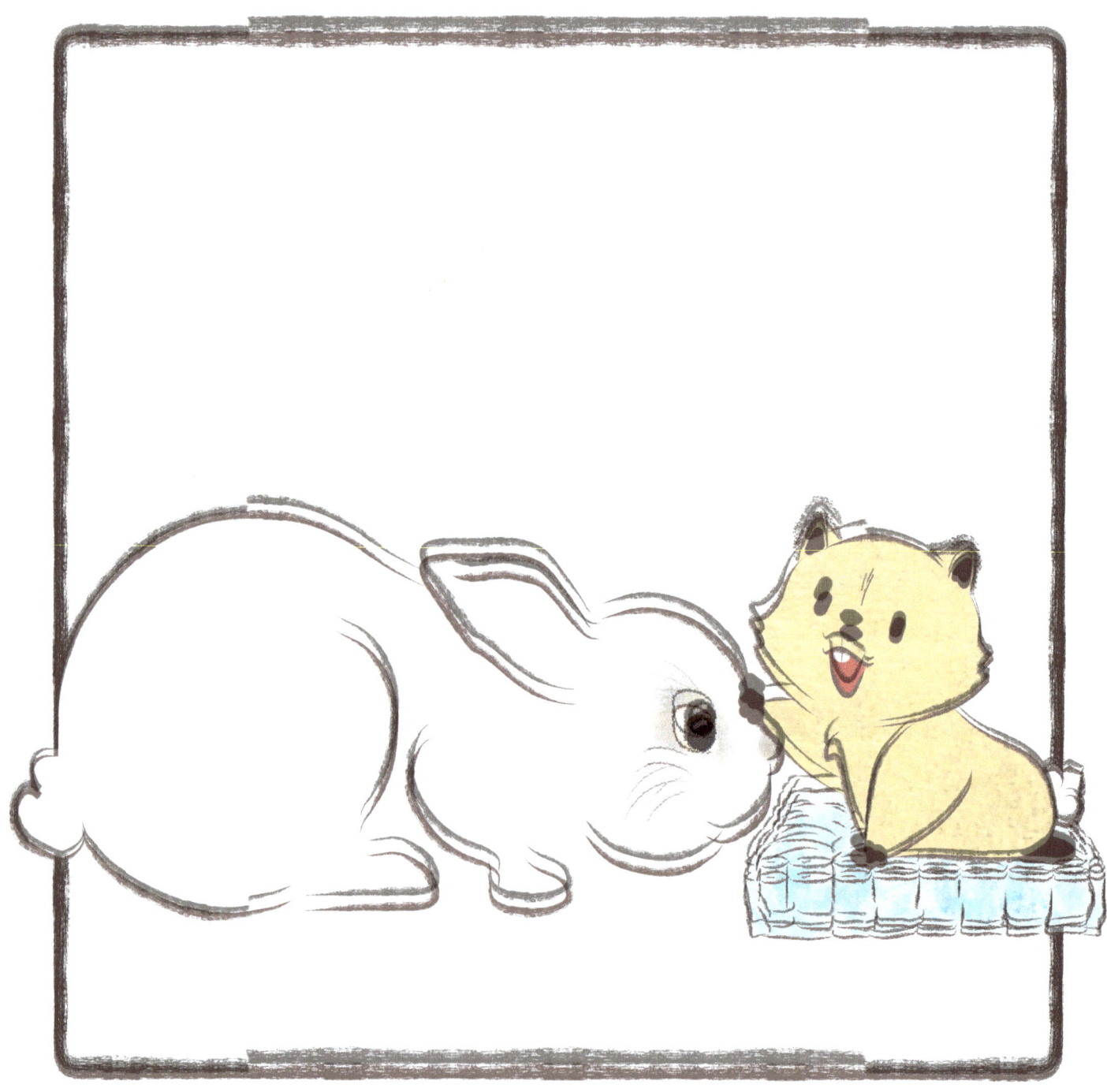

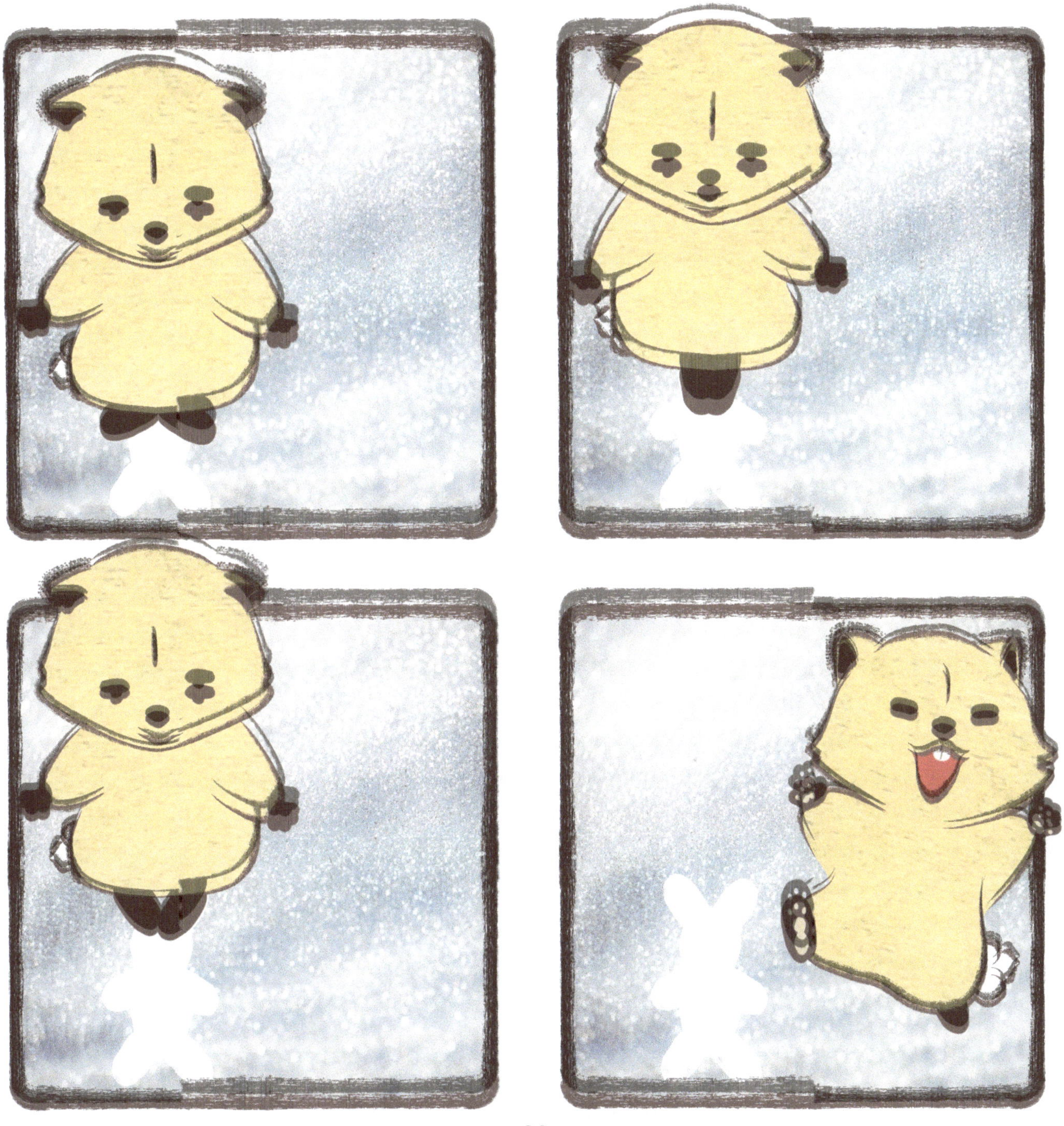

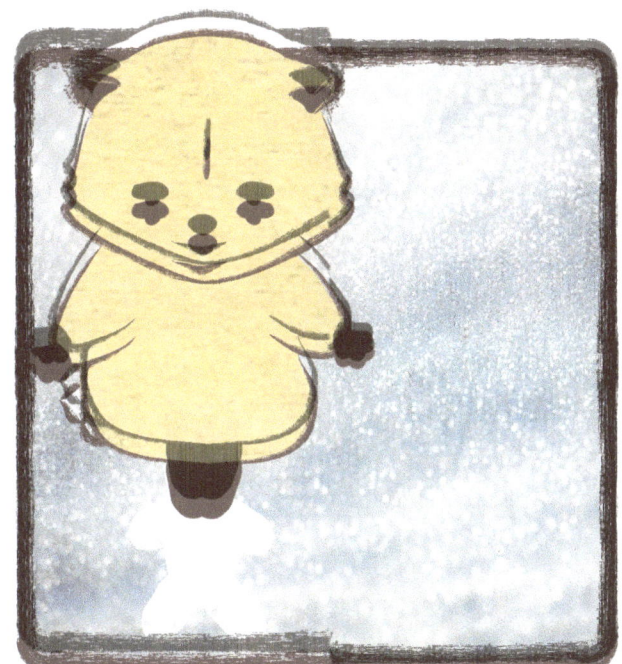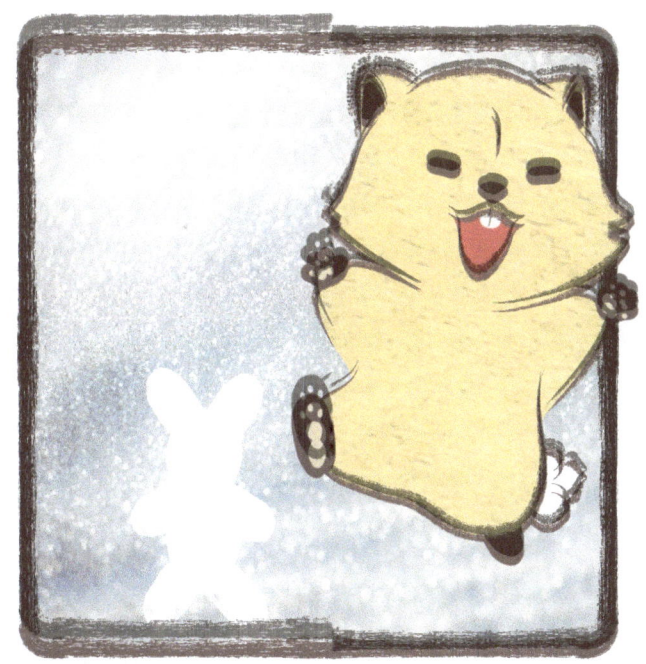

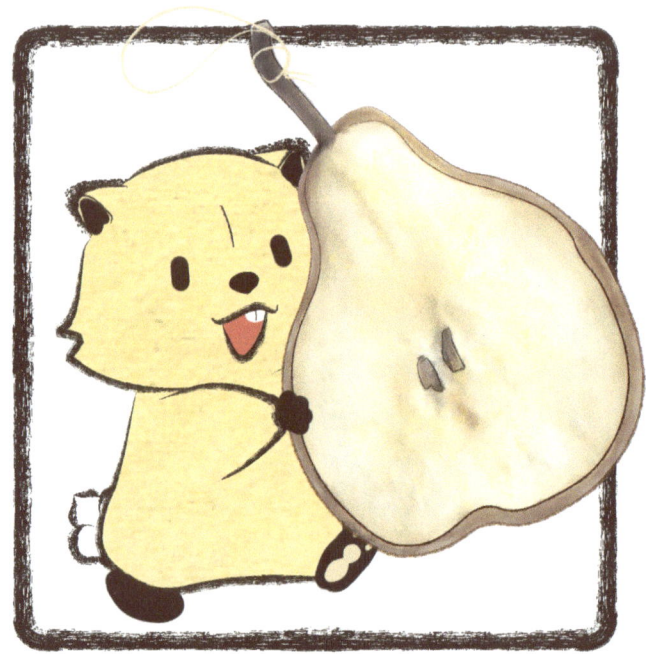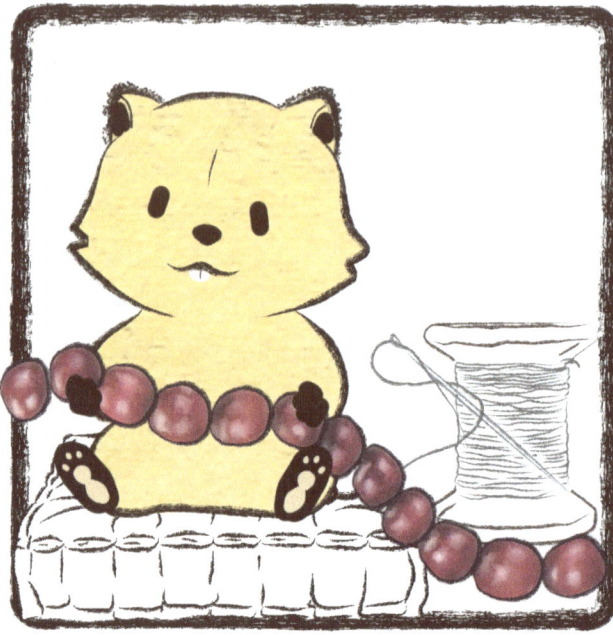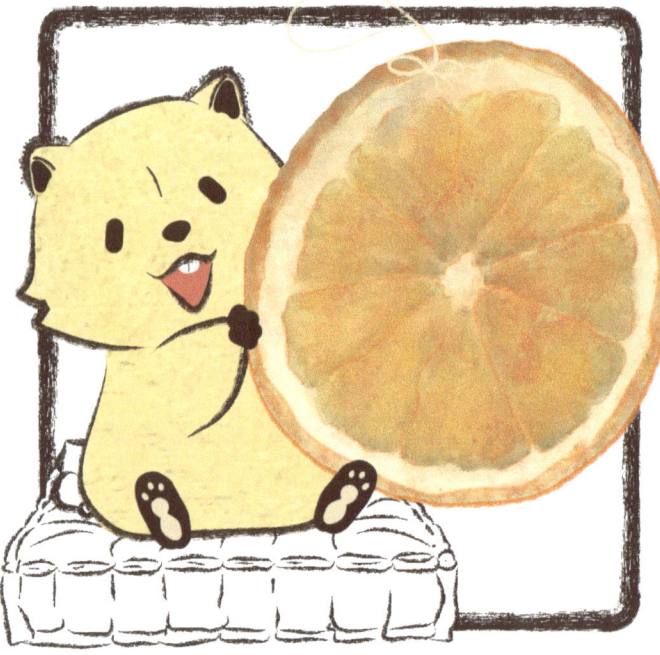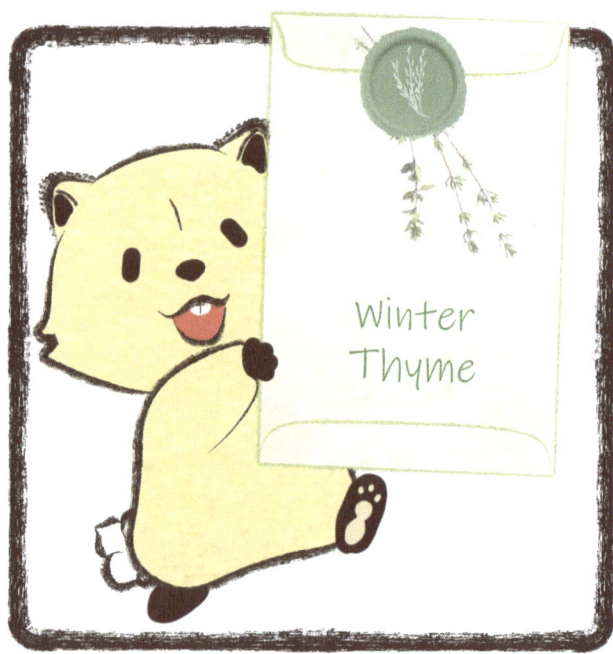

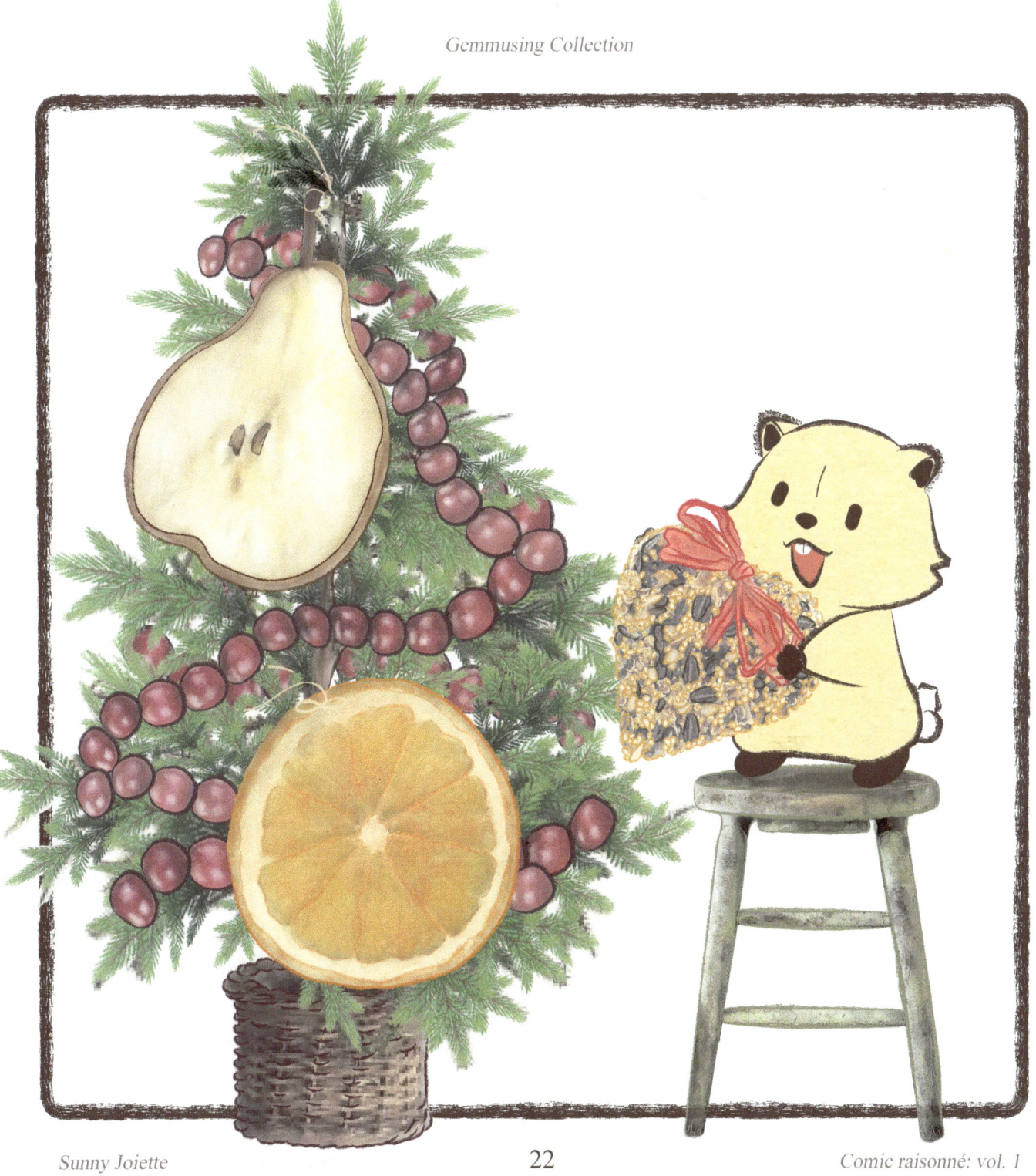

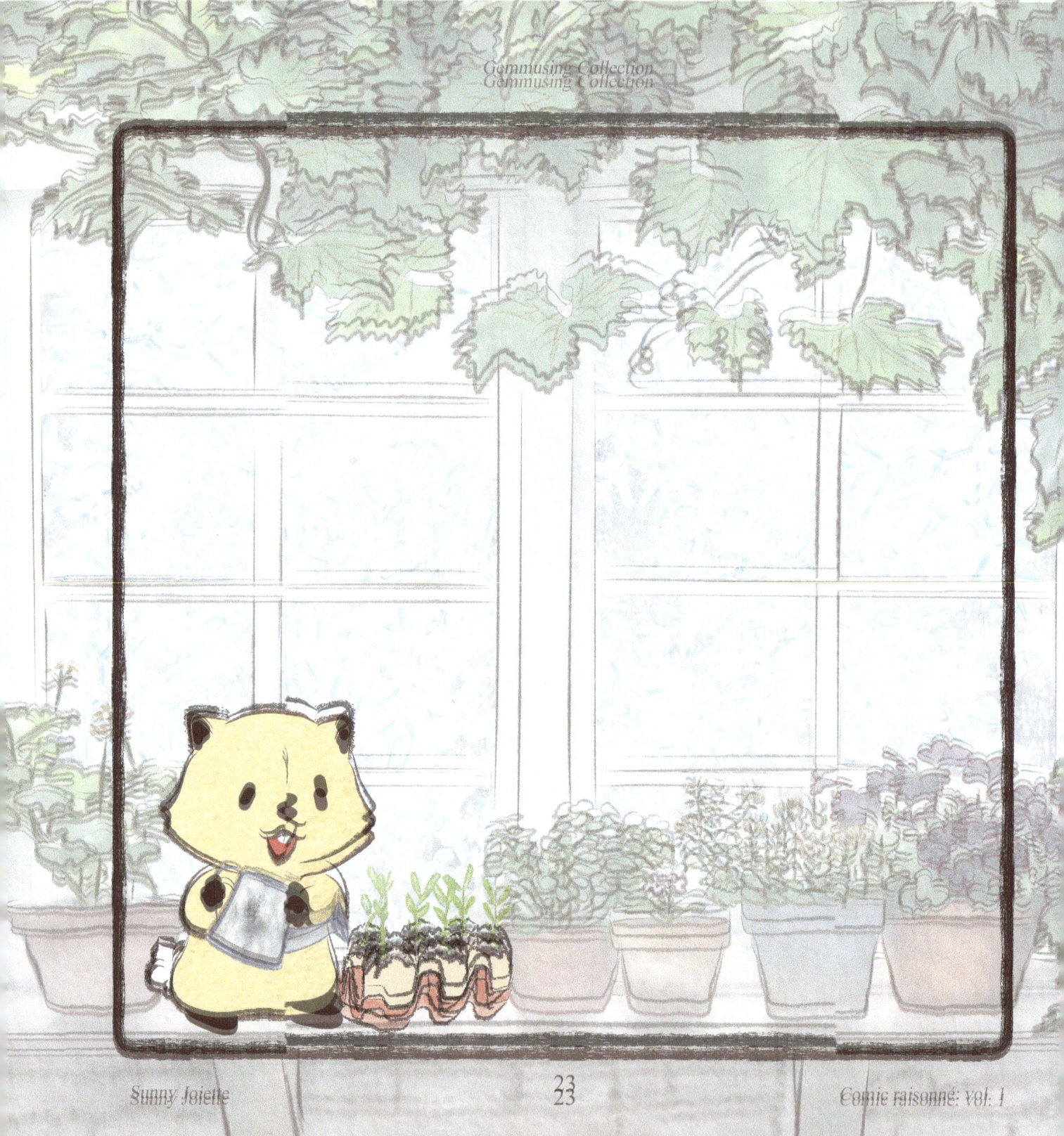

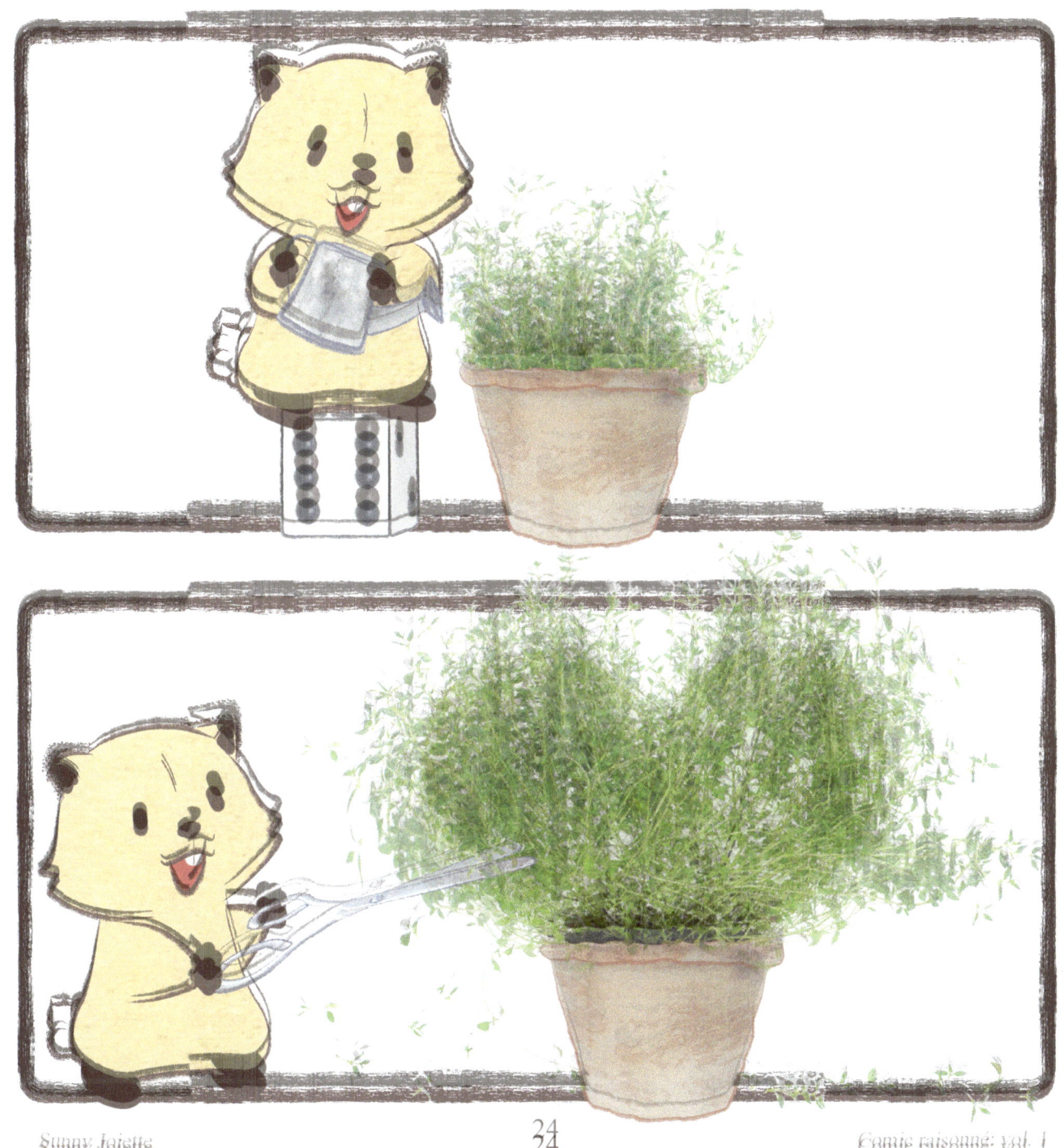

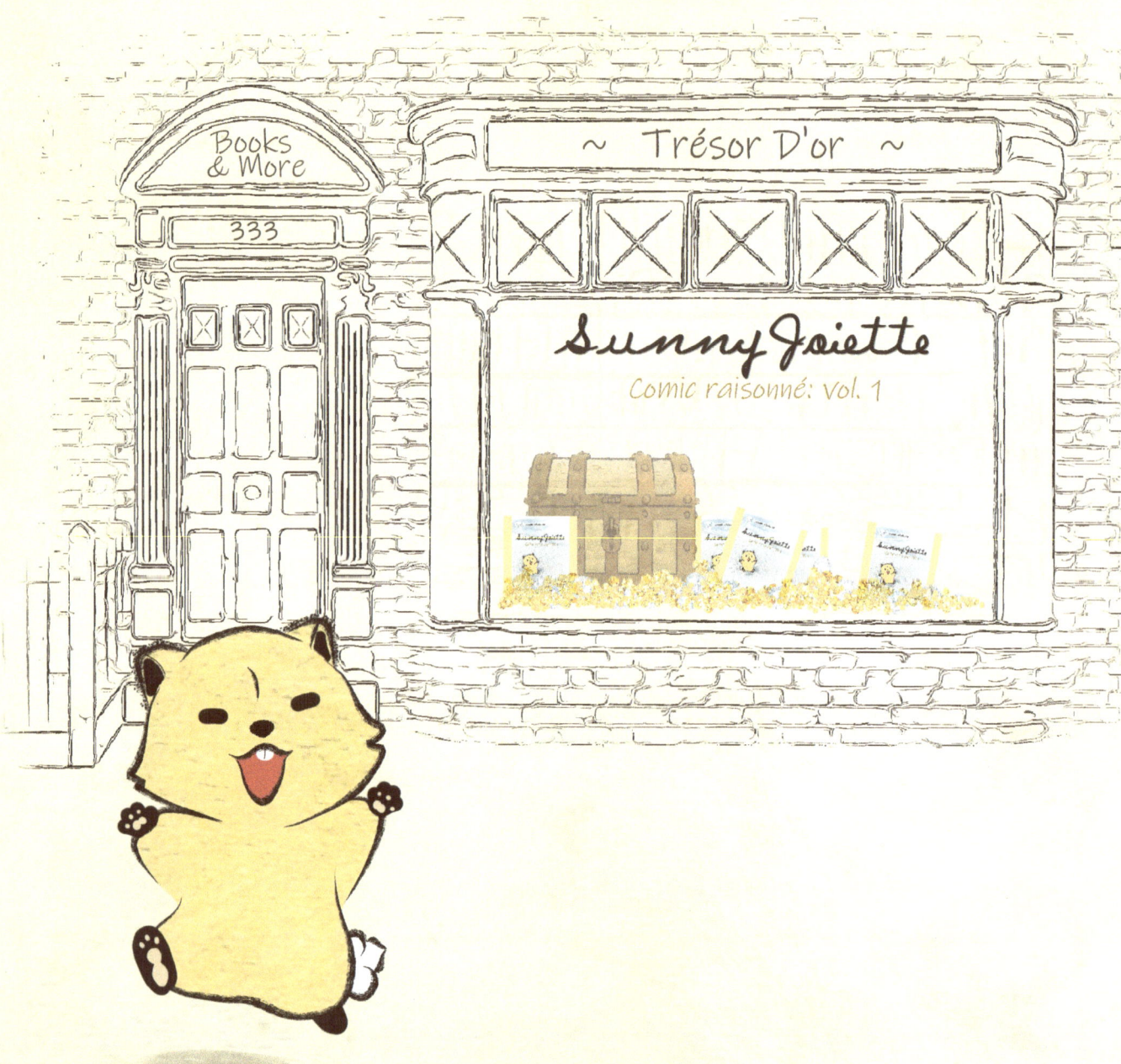

Gemmusing Collection

Book-by-Book,
Gem-by-Gem,
Sunny builds his
Happy Place Treasury
with the Gemmusing Collection.

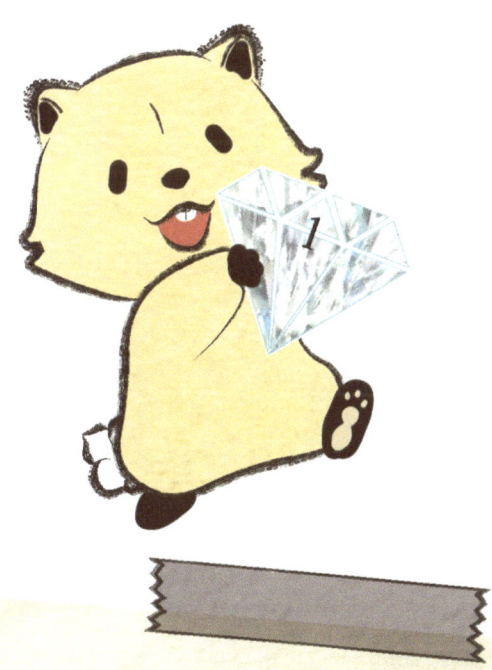

Sunny Joiette   *five*   *Comic raisonné: vol. 1*

Gemmusing Collection
Gemmusing Collection

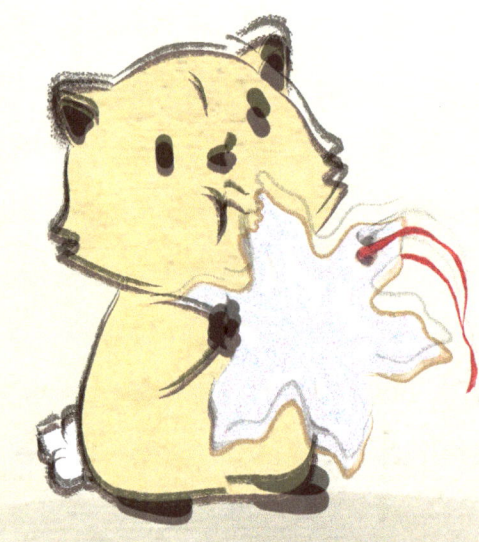

Sunny Joiette six/six Comic raisonné: vol. 1

www.ingramcontent.com/pod-product-compliance
Lightning Source LLC
Chambersburg PA
CBHW051935210526
45473CB00006B/2257